# Mediterranean Diet Cookbook for Weight Loss

*50 Vibrant, Kitchen-Tested Recipes for Living and Eating Well Every Day*

# Sommario

# Introduction

A Mediterranean diet offers a number of health benefits such as controlling and preventing diabetes, improving brain and heart health, preventing cancer and losing weight.

This list of recipes, and ingredients, point right to a healthy eating regimen, to lose weight, without losing the taste of a delicious dish.

I want to help you in this, stay in ideal physical shape, while eating delicious things all the time.

Let's start cooking, and try our best.

# Breakfast & Brunch Recipes

## Green Shakshuka

| Servings: 2 |
| :---: |
| Cooking Time: 15 Minutes |

## Ingredients:

- 1 tbsp olive oil

- 1 onion, peeled and diced

- 1 clove garlic, peeled and finely minced

- 3 cups broccoli rabe, chopped

- 3 cups baby spinach leaves

- 2 tbsp whole milk or cream

- 1 tsp ground cumin

- 1/4 tsp black pepper

- 1/4 tsp salt (or to taste)

- 4 Eggs

- Garnish:

- 1 pinch sea salt

- 1 pinch red pepper flakes

## Directions:

1. Pre-heat the oven to 350 degrees F

2. Add the broccoli rabe to a large pot of boiling water, cook for minutes, drain and set aside

3. In a large oven-proof skillet or cast-iron pan over medium heat, add in the tablespoon of olive oil along with the diced onions, cook for about 10 minutes or until the onions become translucent

4. Add the minced garlic and continue cooking for about another minute

5. Cut the par-cooked broccoli rabe into small pieces, stir into the onion and garlic mixture

6. Cook for a couple of minutes, then stir in the baby spinach leaves, continue to cook for a couple more minutes, stirring often, until the spinach begins to wilt

7. Stir in the ground cumin, salt, ground black pepper, and milk

8. Make four wells in the mixture, crack an egg into each well – be careful not to break the yolks. Also, note that it's easier to crack each egg into a small bowl and then transfer them to the pan

9. Place the pan with the eggs into the pre-heated oven, cook for 10 to 15 minutes until the eggs are set to preference

10. Sprinkle the cooked eggs with a dash of sea salt and a pinch of red pepper flakes

11. Allow to cool, distribute among the containers, store for 2-3 days

12. To Serve: Microwave for 1-minute Or until heated through, serve with crusty whole-wheat bread or warmed slices of pita or naan

---

### Nutrition Info: Per Serving:

- Calories:278;
- Carbs: 18g;
- Total Fat: 16g;
- Protein: 16g

# Clean Breakfast Cookies

| Servings: 4 |
| :---: |
| Cooking Time: 20 Minutes |

## Ingredients:

- 2 cups oats (rolled)
- 1 cup whole wheat flour
- ¼ cup flax seed

- 2½ teaspoons cinnamon (ground)

- 1 cup honey

- ½ teaspoon baking soda

- 2 egg whites

- ½ teaspoon vanilla extract

- 4 tablespoons almond butter

- pinch of salt

**Directions:**

1. Preheat oven to 325 degrees F.

2. Whisk oats, flour, flaxseed, cinnamon, salt, and baking soda together in a bowl.

3. Then, stir honey, egg whites, almond butter, and vanilla extract into the oats mixture until dough is blended.

4. Now, prepare the baking sheets and scoop the dough in them.

5. Finally, bake for about 20 minutes.

6. Serve warm or room temperature.

# Nutrition Info:Per Serving:

- Calories: 686,
- Total Fat: 14.3g,
- Saturated Fat: 1.3,
- Cholesterol: 0 mg,
- Sodium: 185 mg,
- Total Carbohydrate: 131.4 g,
- Dietary Fiber: 11.9 g,
- Total Sugars: .2 g,
- Protein: 15.6 g,
- Vitamin D: 0 mcg,
- Calcium: 100 mg,
- Iron: 9 mg,
- Potassium: 456 mg

# Omelet With Cheese And Broccoli

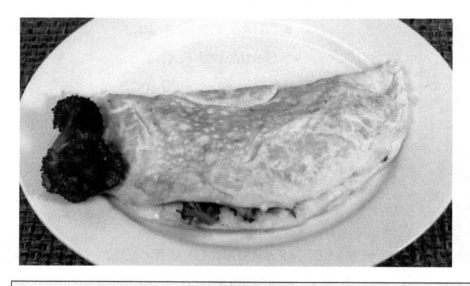

**Servings: 4**

**Cooking Time: 30 Minutes**

**Ingredients:**

- 6 eggs

- 2 ½ cups of broccoli florets

- ¼ cup of milk

- 1 tablespoon olive oil

- ⅓ cup Romano cheese, grated

- ¼ teaspoon pepper

- ⅕ teaspoon salt

- ⅓ cup Greek olives, sliced

- Parsley and more Romano cheese for garnish

## Directions:

1. Turn your oven to broil.

2. Set a steamer basket in a large pan and add 1 inch of water.

3. Add the broccoli to the steamer basket and turn the range to medium. Once the water starts to boil, reduce the temperature to low. Steam the broccoli for 4 to 5 minutes. You will know the vegetable is done when it is soft and tender.

4. In a large bowl, whisk the eggs.

5. Pour in the milk, pepper, and salt.

6. Once the broccoli is done, toss into the large bowl and add the olives and grated cheese.

7. Grease an oven-proof 10-inch skillet and turn the heat on the burner to medium.

8. Add in the egg mixture, then cook for 4 to 5 minutes.

9. Set the skillet into the oven but make sure it's at least 4 inches from the heating source. Broil the eggs for 3 minutes. If the eggs are not completely set, continue cooking for another minute or two.

10. Remove the eggs from the oven and set on the stove so they can cool for a few minutes.

11. Garnish the omelet with cheese and parsley. Then, cut into wedges and  enjoy!

---

**Nutrition Info:**

- calories: 229,
- fats: 17 grams,

- carbohydrates: 5 grams,
- protein: 15 grams.

# Greek Yogurt Breakfast Bowl

## Ingredients:

- 1 cup Greek Yogurt plain
- 13 cup Pomegranate Seeds (or fresh fruit of your choice)
- 1 tsp honey

## Directions:

1. In a jar with a lid, add the Greek yogurt in a bowl top with fruit and drizzle honey over the top

2. Close the lid and refrigerate for 3 days

## Nutrition Info: Per Serving:

- Calories116;
- Carbs 24g;
- Total Fat 1.2g;
- Protein 4g

# Cucumber Celery Lime Smoothie

| |
|---|
| **Servings: 2** |
| **Cooking Time: 15 Minutes** |

## Ingredients:

- 8 stalks of celery, chopped

- 1 lemon, juiced

- 2 cucumbers, peeled and chopped

- ½ cup ice

- sweetener of your choice

- 1 cup water

**Directions:**

1. Place all the Ingredients: in a blender.

2. Blend well until smooth and frothy or desired texture.

3. Serve chilled.

4. Enjoy.

---

- **Nutrition Info: Per Serving:**
- Calories: 64,
- Total Fat: 0.,
- Saturated Fat: 0.2,
- Cholesterol: 0 mg,
- Sodium: 63 mg,
- Total Carbohydrate: 15.7 g,
- Dietary Fiber: 3.4 g,

- Total Sugars: 6.7 g,
- Protein: 2.8 g,
- Vitamin D: 0 mcg,
- Calcium: 85 mg,
- Iron: 1 mg,
- Potassium: 660 mg

# Chocolate-almond Banana Bread

| Servings: 4 |
| --- |
| Cooking Time: 25 Minutes |

**Ingredients:**

- Cooking spray or oil to grease the pan

- 1 cup almond meal

- 2 large eggs

- 2 very ripe bananas, mashed

- 1 tablespoon plus 2 teaspoons maple syrup

- ½ teaspoon vanilla extract

- ½ teaspoon baking powder

- ¼ teaspoon ground cardamom

- ⅓ cup dark chocolate chips, very roughly chopped

**Directions:**

1. Preheat the oven to 350°F and spray an 8-inch cake pan or baking dish with cooking spray or rub with oil.

2. Combine all the ingredients in a large mixing bowl. Then pour the mixture into the prepared pan.

3. Place the pan in the oven and bake for 25 minutes. The edges should be browned, and a paring knife should come out clean when the banana bread is pierced.

4. When cool, slice into wedges and place 1 wedge in each of 4 containers.

5. STORAGE: Store covered containers at room temperature for up to 2 days, refrigerate for up to 7 days, or freeze for up to 3 months.

---

**Nutrition Info: Per Serving:**

- Total calories: 3;
- Total fat: 23g;
- Saturated fat: 6g;
- Sodium: 105mg;
- Carbohydrates: 37g;
- Fiber: 6g;
- Protein: 10g

# Mediterranean Breakfast Egg White Sandwich

| Servings: 1 |
| --- |
| Cooking Time: 30 Minutes |

**Ingredients:**

- 1 tsp vegan butter

- ¼ cup egg whites

- 1 tsp chopped fresh herbs such as parsley, basil, rosemary

- 1 whole grain seeded ciabatta roll

- 1 tbsp pesto

- 1-2 slices muenster cheese (or other cheese such as provolone, Monterey Jack, etc.)

- About ½ cup roasted tomatoes

- Salt, to taste

- Pepper, to taste

- Roasted Tomatoes:

- 10 oz grape tomatoes

- 1 tbsp extra virgin olive oil

- Kosher salt, to taste

- Coarse black pepper, to taste

## Directions:

1. In a small nonstick skillet over medium heat, melt the vegan butter

2. Pour in egg whites, season with salt and pepper, sprinkle with fresh herbs, cook for 3-4 minutes or until egg is done, flip once

3. In the meantime, toast the ciabatta bread in toaster

4. Once done, spread both halves with pesto

5. Place the egg on the bottom half of sandwich roll, folding if necessary, top with cheese, add the roasted tomatoes and top half of roll sandwich

6. To make the roasted tomatoes: Preheat oven to 400 degrees F. Slice tomatoes in half lengthwise. Then place them onto a baking sheet and drizzle with the olive oil, toss to coat. Season with salt and pepper and roast in oven

for about 20 minutes, until the skin appears wrinkled

---

## Nutrition Info: Per Serving:

- Calories:458;
- Total Carbohydrates: 51g;
- Total Fat: 0g;Protein: 21g

# Strawberry-apricot Smoothie

**Servings: 2**

**Cooking Time: 15 Minutes**

## Ingredients:

- 1 cup strawberries, frozen

- ¾ cup almond milk, unsweetened

- 2 apricots, pitted and sliced

## Directions:

1. Put all the Ingredients: into the blender.

2. Blend them for a minute or until you reach desired foamy texture.

3. Serve the smoothie.

4. Enjoy.

## Nutrition Info: Per Serving:

- Calories: 247,
- Total Fat: 21.9 g,
- Saturated Fat: 19 g,
- Cholesterol: 0 mg,
- Sodium: 1mg,
- Total Carbohydrate: 14.4 g,
- Dietary Fiber: 4.1 g,
- Total Sugars: 9.7 g,
- Protein: 3 g,
- Vitamin D: 0 mcg,
- Calcium: 30 mg,
- Iron: 2 mg,
- Potassium: 438 mg

# Apple Quinoa Breakfast Bars

| |
|---|
| **Servings: 12** |
| **Cooking Time: 40 Minutes** |

**Ingredients:**

- 2 eggs

- 1 apple peeled and chopped into ½ inch chunks

- 1 cup unsweetened apple sauce

- 1 ½ cups cooked & cooled quinoa

- 1 ½ cups rolled oats

- 1/4 cup peanut butter

- 1 tsp vanilla

- 1/2 tsp cinnamon

- 1/4 cup coconut oil

- ½ tsp baking powder

**Directions:**

1. Heat oven to 350 degrees F

2. Spray an 8x8 inch baking dish with oil, set aside

3. In a large bowl, stir together the apple sauce, cinnamon, coconut oil, peanut butter, vanilla and eggs

4. Add in the cooked quinoa, rolled oats and baking powder, mix until completely incorporated

5. Fold in the apple chunks

6. Spread the mixture into the prepared baking dish, spreading it to each corner

7. Bake for 40 minutes, or until a toothpick comes out clean

8. Allow to cool before slicing

9. Wrap the bars individually in plastic wrap. Store in an airtight container or baggie in the freezer for up to a month.

10. To serve: Warm up in the oven at 350 F for 5 minutes or microwave for up to 30 seconds

---

**Nutrition Info: Per Serving:** (1 bar):

- Calories:230;
- Total Fat: 10g;
- Total Carbs: 31g;
- Protein: 7g

# Pepper, Kale, And Chickpea Shakshuka

| Servings: 5 |
| --- |
| Cooking Time: 35 Minutes |

**Ingredients:**

- 1 tablespoon olive oil

- 1 small red onion, thinly sliced

- 1 red bell pepper, thinly sliced

- 1 green bell pepper, thinly sliced

- 1 bunch kale, stemmed and roughly chopped

- ½ cup packed cilantro leaves, chopped

- ½ teaspoon kosher salt

- 1 teaspoon smoked paprika

- 1 (14.5-ounce) can diced tomatoes

- 1 (14-ounce) can low-sodium chickpeas, drained and rinsed

- ⅔ cup water

- 5 eggs

- 2½ whole-wheat pitas (optional)

**Directions:**

1. Preheat the oven to 375°F.

2. Heat the oil in an oven-safe 1inch skillet over medium-high heat. Once the oil is shimmering, add the onions and red and green bell peppers. Sauté for 5 minutes, then cover, leaving the lid slightly ajar. Cook for 5 more minutes, then add the kale and cover, leaving the lid slightly ajar. Cook for 10 more minutes, stirring occasionally.

3. Add the cilantro, salt, paprika, tomatoes, chickpeas, and water, and stir to combine.

4. Make 5 wells in the mixture. Break an egg into a small bowl and pour it into a well. Repeat with the remaining eggs.

5. Place the pan in the oven and bake until the egg whites are opaque and the eggs still jiggle a little when the pan is shaken, about 12 to 1minutes, but start checking at 8 minutes.

6. When the shakshuka is cool, scoop about 1¼ cups of veggies into each of 5 containers, along with 1 egg each. If using, place ½ pita in each of 5 resealable bags.

7. STORAGE: Store covered containers in the refrigerator for up to 5 days.

---

## Nutrition Info: Per Serving:

- Total calories: 244;
- Total fat: 9g;
- Saturated fat: 2g;
- Sodium: 529mg;
- Carbohydrates: 29g;
- Fiber: ;
- Protein: 14g

# Rosemary Broccoli Cauliflower Mash

**Servings: 3**

**Cooking Time: 12 Minutes**

**Ingredients:**

- 2 cups broccoli, chopped

- 1 lb cauliflower, cut into florets

- 1 tsp dried rosemary

- 1/4 cup olive oil

- 1 tsp garlic, minced

- Salt

**Directions:**

1. Add broccoli and cauliflower into the instant pot. Pour enough water into the pot to cover broccoli and cauliflower.

2. Seal pot with lid and cook on high for 1minutes.

3. Once done, allow to release pressure naturally. Remove lid.

4. Drain broccoli and cauliflower well and clean the instant pot.

5. Add oil into the pot and set the pot on sauté mode.

6. Add broccoli, cauliflower, rosemary, garlic, and salt and cook for 10 minutes.

7. Mash the broccoli and cauliflower mixture using a potato masher until smooth.

8. Serve and enjoy.

**Nutrition Info:**

- Calories: 205;

- Fat: 17.2 g;
- Carbohydrates: 12.6 g;
- Sugar: 4.7 g;
- Protein: 4.8 g;
- Cholesterol: 0 mg

# Lunch and Dinner Recipes

## Bacon Wrapped Asparagus

Servings: 2

Cooking Time: 30 Minutes

## Ingredients:

- 1/3 cup heavy whipping cream

- 2 bacon slices, precooked

- 4 small spears asparagus

- Salt, to taste

- 1 tablespoon butter

## Directions:

1. Preheat the oven to 360 degrees F and grease a baking sheet with butter.

2. Meanwhile, mix cream, asparagus and salt in a bowl.

3. Wrap the asparagus in bacon slices and arrange them in the baking dish.

4. Transfer the baking dish in the oven and bake for about 20 minutes.

5. Remove from the oven and serve hot.

6. Place the bacon wrapped asparagus in a dish and set aside to cool for meal prepping. Divide it in 2 containers and cover the lid. Refrigerate for about 2 days and reheat in the microwave before serving.

---

**Nutrition Info:**

- Calories: 204 ;
- Carbohydrates: 1.4g;
- Protein: 5.9g;
- Fat: 19.3g;
- Sugar: 0.5g;
- Sodium: 291mg

# Cool Mediterranean Fish

**Servings: 8**

**Cooking Time: 30 Minutes**

## Ingredients:

- 6 ounces halibut fillets

- 1 tablespoon Greek seasoning

- 1 large tomato, chopped

- 1 onion, chopped

- 5 ounces kalamata olives, pitted

- ¼ cup capers

- ¼ cup olive oil

- 1 tablespoon lemon juice

- Salt and pepper as needed

## Directions:

1. Pre-heat your oven to 350-degree Fahrenheit

2. Transfer the halibut fillets on a large aluminum foil

3. Season with Greek seasoning

4. Take a bowl and add tomato, onion, olives, olive oil, capers, pepper, lemon juice and salt

5. Mix well and spoon the tomato mix over the halibut

6. Seal the edges and fold to make a packet

7. Place the packet on a baking sheet and bake in your oven for 30-40 minutes

8. Serve once the fish flakes off and enjoy!

9. Meal Prep/Storage Options: Store in airtight containers in your fridge for 1-2 days.

## Nutrition Info:

- Calories: 429;
- Fat: 26g;
- Carbohydrates: ;
- Protein:36g

# Luncheon Fancy Salad

| Servings: 2 |
|---|
| Cooking Time: 40 Minutes |

**Ingredients:**

- 6-ounce cooked salmon, chopped

- 1 tablespoon fresh dill, chopped

- Salt and black pepper, to taste

- 4 hard-boiled grass-fed eggs, peeled and cubed

- 2 celery stalks, chopped

- ½ yellow onion, chopped

- ¾ cup avocado mayonnaise

**Directions:**

1. Put all the ingredients in a bowl and mix until well combined.

2. Cover with a plastic wrap and refrigerate for about 3 hours to serve.

3. For meal prepping, put the salad in a container and refrigerate for up to days.

**Nutrition Info:**

- Calories: 303 ;
- Carbohydrates: 1.7g;
- Protein: 10.3g;
- Fat: 30g ;
- Sugar: 1g;
- Sodium: 31g

# Moroccan Spiced Stir-fried Beef With Butternut Squash And Chickpeas

**Ingredients:**

- 1 tablespoon olive oil, plus 2 teaspoons

- 1 pound precut butternut squash cut into ½-inch cubes

- 3 ounces scallions, white and green parts chopped (1 cup)

- 1 tablespoon water

- ¼ teaspoon baking soda

- ¾ pound flank steak, sliced across the grain into ⅛-inch thick slices

- ½ teaspoon garlic powder

- ¼ teaspoon ground ginger

- ¼ teaspoon turmeric

- ¼ teaspoon ground cumin

- ¼ teaspoon ground coriander

- ⅛ teaspoon cayenne pepper

- ⅛ teaspoon ground cinnamon

- ½ teaspoon kosher salt, divided

- 1 (14-ounce) can chickpeas, drained and rinsed

- ½ cup dried apricots, quartered

- ½ cup cilantro leaves, chopped

- 2 teaspoons freshly squeezed lemon juice

- 8 teaspoons sliced almonds

## Directions:

1. Heat tablespoon of oil in a 12-inch skillet. Once the oil is hot, add the squash and scallions, and cook until the squash is tender, about 10 to 12 minutes.

2. Mix the water and baking soda together in a small prep bowl. Place the beef in a medium bowl, pour the baking-soda water over it, and mix to combine. Let it sit for 5 minutes.

3. In a small bowl, combine the garlic powder, ginger, turmeric, cumin, coriander, cayenne, cinnamon, and ¼ teaspoon of salt, then add the mixture to the beef. Stir to combine.

4. When the squash is tender, turn the heat off and add the remaining ¼ teaspoon of salt and the chickpeas, dried apricots, cilantro, and lemon juice to taste. Stir to combine. Place the contents of the pan in a bowl to cool.

5. Clean out the skillet and heat the remaining 2 teaspoons of oil over high heat. When the oil is

hot, add the beef and cook until it is no longer pink, about 2 to 3 minutes.

6. Place 1¼ cups of the squash mixture and one quarter of the beef slices in each of 4 containers. Sprinkle 2 teaspoons of sliced almonds over each container.

7. STORAGE: Store covered containers in the refrigerator for up to 5 days.

**Nutrition Info: Per Serving:**

- Total calories: 404;
- Total fat: 14g;
- Saturated fat: 1g;
- Sodium: 355mg;
- Carbohydrates: 46g;
- Fiber: 12g;
- Protein: 27g

# North African–inspired Sautéed Shrimp With Leeks And Peppers

| |
|---|
| **Servings: 4** |
| **Cooking Time: 20 Minutes** |

**Ingredients:**

- 2 tablespoons olive oil, divided

- 1 large leek, white and light green parts, halved lengthwise, sliced ¼-inch thick

- 2 teaspoons chopped garlic

- 1 large red bell pepper, chopped into ¼-inch pieces

- 1 cup chopped fresh parsley leaves (1 small bunch)

- ½ cup chopped fresh cilantro leaves (½ small bunch)

- ¼ teaspoon ground cumin

- ¼ teaspoon ground coriander

- 1 teaspoon smoked paprika

- 1 pound uncooked peeled, deveined large shrimp (20 to 25 per pound), thawed if frozen, blotted with paper towels

- 1 tablespoon freshly squeezed lemon juice

- ⅛ teaspoon kosher salt

**Directions:**

1. Heat 2 teaspoons of oil in a -inch skillet over medium heat. Once the oil is hot, add the leeks and garlic and sauté for 2 minutes. Add the peppers and cook for 10 minutes, or until the peppers are soft, stirring occasionally.

2. Add the chopped parsley and cilantro and cook for 1 more minute. Remove the mixture from the pan and place in a medium bowl.

3. Mix the cumin, coriander, and paprika in a small prep bowl.

4. Add 2 teaspoons of oil to the same skillet and increase the heat to medium-high. Add the shrimp in a single layer, sprinkle the spice mixture over the shrimp, and cook for about 2 minutes. Flip the shrimp over and cook for 1 more minute. Add the leek and herb mixture, stir, and cook for 1 more minute.

5. Turn off the heat and add the remaining 2 teaspoons of oil and the lemon juice. Taste to see whether you need the salt. Add if necessary.

6. Place ¾ cup of couscous or other grain (if using) and 1 cup of the shrimp mixture in each of 4 containers.

7. STORAGE: Store covered containers in the refrigerator for up to 4 days.

**Nutrition Info: Per Serving:**

- Total calories: 1;
- Total fat: 9g;
- Saturated fat: 1g;
- Sodium: 403mg;
- Carbohydrates: 9g;
- Fiber: 2g;
- Protein: 19g

# Italian Chicken With Sweet Potato And Broccoli

**Servings: 8**

**Cooking Time: 30 Minutes**

## Ingredients:

- 2 lbs boneless skinless chicken breasts, cut into small pieces

- 5-6 cups broccoli florets

- 3 tbsp Italian seasoning mix of your choice

- a few tbsp of olive oil

- 3 sweet potatoes, peeled and diced

- Coarse sea salt, to taste

- Freshly cracked pepper, to taste

- Toppings:

- Avocado

- Lemon juice

- Chives

- Olive oil, for serving

## Directions:

1. Preheat the oven to 425 degrees F

2. Toss the chicken pieces with the Italian seasoning mix and a drizzle of olive oil, stir to combine then store in the fridge for about 30 minutes

3. Arrange the broccoli florets and sweet potatoes on a sheet pan, drizzle with the olive oil, sprinkle generously with salt

4. Arrange the chicken on a separate sheet pan

5. Bake both in the oven for 12-1minutes

6. Transfer the chicken and broccoli to a plate, toss the sweet potatoes and continue to roast for another 15 minutes, or until ready

7. Allow the chicken, broccoli, and sweet potatoes to cool

8. Distribute among the containers and store for 2-3 days

9. To Serve: Reheat in the microwave for 1 minute or until heated through, top with the topping of choice. Enjoy

10. Recipe Notes: Any kind of vegetables work will with this recipe! So, add favorites like carrots, brussels sprouts and asparagus.

---

**Nutrition Info: Per Serving:**

- Calories:222;
- Total Fat: 4.9g;
- Total Carbs: 15.3g;
- Protein: 28g

# Vegetable Soup

**Servings: 6**

**Cooking Time: 20 Minutes**

**Ingredients:**

- 1 15-ounce can low sodium cannellini beans, drained and rinsed

- 1 tablespoon olive oil

- 1 small onion, diced

- 2 carrots, diced

- 2 stalks celery, diced

- 1 small zucchini, diced

- 1 garlic clove, minced

- 1 tablespoon fresh thyme leaves, chopped

- 2 teaspoons fresh sage, chopped

- ½ teaspoon salt

- ¼ teaspoon freshly ground black pepper

- 32 ounces low sodium chicken broth

- 1 14-ounce can no-salt diced tomatoes, undrained

- 2 cups baby spinach leaves, chopped

- 1/3 cup freshly grated parmesan

**Directions:**

1. Mash half of the beans in a small bowl using the back of a spoon and put it to the side.

2. Add the oil to a large soup pot and place over medium-high heat.

3. Add carrots, onion, celery, garlic, zucchini, thyme, salt, pepper, and sage.

4. Cook well for about 5 minutes until the vegetables are tender.

5. Add broth and tomatoes and bring the mixture to a boil.

6. Add beans (both mashed and whole) and spinach.

7. Cook for 3 minutes until the spinach has wilted.

8. Pour the soup into the jars.

9. Before serving, top with parmesan.

10. Enjoy!

## Nutrition Info: Per Serving:

- Calories: 359,
- Total Fat: 7.1 g,
- Saturated Fat: 2.7 g,
- Cholesterol: 10 mg,
- Sodium: 854 mg,
- Total Carbohydrate: 51.1 g,

- Dietary Fiber: 20 g,
- Total Sugars: 5.7 g,
- Protein: 25.8 g,
- Vitamin D: 0 mcg,
- Calcium: 277 mg,
- Iron: 7 mg,
- Potassium: 1497 mg

# Greek Chicken Wraps

| |
|---|
| **Servings: 2** |
| **Cooking Time: 15 Minutes** |

## Ingredients:

- Greek Chicken Wrap Filling:

- 2 chicken breasts 14 oz, chopped into 1-inch pieces

- 2 small zucchinis, cut into 1-inch pieces

- 2 bell peppers, cut into 1-inch pieces

- 1 red onion, cut into 1-inch pieces

- 2 tbsp olive oil

- 2 tsp oregano

- 2 tsp basil

- 1/2 tsp garlic powder

- 1/2 tsp onion powder

- 1/2 tsp salt

- 2 lemons, sliced

- To Serve:

- 1/4 cup feta cheese crumbled

- 4 large flour tortillas or wraps

## Directions:

1. Pre-heat oven to 425 degrees F

2. In a bowl, toss together the chicken, zucchinis, olive oil, oregano, basil, garlic, bell peppers, onion powder, onion powder and salt

3. Arrange lemon slice on the baking sheet(s), spread the chicken and vegetable out on top (use 2 baking sheets if needed)

4. Bake for 15 minutes, until veggies are soft and the chicken is cooked through

5. Allow to cool completely

6. Distribute the chicken, bell pepper, zucchini and onions among the containers and remove the lemon slices

7. Allow the dish to cool completely

8. Distribute among the containers, store for 3 days

9. To Serve: Reheat in the microwave for 1-2 minutes or until heated through. Wrap in a tortila and sprinkle with feta cheese. Enjoy!

**Nutrition Info: Per Serving:** (1 wrap):

- Calories:356;
- Total Fat: 14g;
- Total Carbs: 26g;
- Protein: 29g

# Garbanzo Bean Soup

**Servings: 4**

**Cooking Time: 20 Minutes**

**Ingredients:**

- 14 ounces diced tomatoes

- 1 teaspoon olive oil

- 1 15-ounce can garbanzo beans

- salt

- pepper

- 2 sprigs fresh rosemary

- 1 cup acini di pepe pasta

**Directions:**

1. Take a large saucepan and add tomatoes and  ounces of the beans.

2. Bring the mixture to a boil over medium-high heat.

3. Puree the remaining beans in a blender/food processor.

4. Stir the pureed mixture into the pan.

5. Add the sprigs of rosemary to the pan.

6. Add acini de Pepe pasta and simmer until the pasta is soft, making sure to stir it from time to time.

7. Remove the rosemary.

8. Season with pepper and salt.

9. Enjoy!

**Nutrition Info: Per Serving:**

- Calories: 473,
- Total Fat: 8.6 g,
- Saturated Fat: 1.1 g,
- Cholesterol: 18 mg,
- Sodium: 66 mg,
- Total Carbohydrate: 78.8 g,
- Dietary Fiber: 19.9 g,
- Total Sugars: 14 g,
- Protein: 23.7 g,
- Vitamin D: 0 mcg,
- Calcium: 131 mg,
- Iron: 8 mg,
- Potassium: 1186 mg

# Spinach And Beans Mediterranean Style Salad

| |
|---|
| **Servings: 4** |
| **Cooking Time: 30 Minutes** |

**Ingredients:**

- 15 ounces drained and rinsed cannellini beans

- 14 ounces drained, rinsed, and quartered artichoke hearts

- 6 ounces or 8 cups baby spinach

- 14 ½ ounces undrained diced tomatoes, no salt is best

- 1 tablespoon olive oil and any additional if you prefer

- ¼ teaspoon salt

- 2 minced garlic cloves

- 1 chopped onion, small in size

- ¼ teaspoon pepper

- ⅛ teaspoon crushed red pepper flakes

- 2 tablespoons Worcestershire sauce

## Directions:

1. Place a saucepan on your stovetop and turn the temperature to medium-high.

2. Let the pan warm up for a minute before you pour in the tablespoon of oil. Continue to let the oil heat up for another minute or two.

3. Toss in your chopped onion and stir so all the pieces are bathed in oil. Saute the onions for minutes.

4. Add the garlic to the saucepan. Stir and saute the ingredients for another minute.

5. Combine the salt, red pepper flakes, pepper, and Worcestershire sauce. Mix well and then

add the tomatoes to the pan. Stir the mixture constantly for about minutes.

6. Add the artichoke hearts, spinach, and beans. Saute and stir occasionally to get the taste throughout the dish. Once the spinach starts to wilt, take the salad off of the heat.

7. Serve and enjoy immediately to get the best taste.

**Nutrition Info:**

- calories: 1,
- fats: 4 grams,
- carbohydrates: 30 grams,
- protein: 8 grams.

# Salmon Skillet Dinner

| |
|---|
| **Servings: 4** |
| **Cooking Time: 15 To 20 Minutes** |

## Ingredients:

- 1 teaspoon minced garlic

- 1 ½ cup quartered cherry tomatoes

- 1 tablespoon water

- ¼ teaspoon sea salt

- 1 tablespoon lemon juice, freshly squeezed is best

- 1 tablespoon extra virgin olive oil

- 12 ounces drained and chopped roasted red peppers

- 1 teaspoon paprika

- ¼ teaspoon black pepper

- 1 pound salmon fillets

## Directions:

1. Remove the skin from your salmon fillets and cut them into 8 pieces.

2. Turn your stove burner on medium heat and set a skillet on top.

3. Pour the olive oil into the skillet and let it heat up for a couple of minutes.

4. Add the minced garlic and paprika. Saute the ingredients for 1 minute.

5. Combine the roasted peppers, black pepper, tomatoes, water, and salt.

6. Set the heat to medium-high and bring the ingredients to a simmer. This should take 3 to 4 minutes. Remember to stir the ingredients occasionally so the tomatoes don't burn.

7. Add the salmon and take some of the sauce from the skillet to spoon on top of the fish so it is all covered in the mixture.

8. Cover the skillet and set a timer for 10 minutes. When the fish reaches 145 degrees Fahrenheit, it is cooked thoroughly.

9. Turn off the heat and drizzle lemon juice over the fish.

10. Break up the salmon into chunks and gently mix the pieces of fish with the sauce.

11. Serve and enjoy!

---

## Nutrition Info:

- calories: 289,
- fats: 13 grams,
- carbohydrates: 10 grams,
- protein: 31 grams.

# Herb-crusted Halibut

| Servings: 4 |
| :---: |
| Cooking Time: 25 Minutes |

## Ingredients:

- Fresh parsley (.33 cup)

- Fresh dill (.25 cup)

- Fresh chives (.25 cup)

- Lemon zest (1 tsp.)

- Panko breadcrumbs (.75 cup)

- Olive oil (1 tbsp.)

- Freshly cracked black pepper (.25 tsp.)

- Sea salt (1 tsp.)

- Halibut fillets (4 - 6 oz.)

**Directions:**

1. Chop the fresh dill, chives, and parsley. Prepare a baking tray using a sheet of foil. Set the oven to reach 400° Fahrenheit.

2. Combine the salt, pepper, lemon zest, olive oil, chives, dill, parsley, and the breadcrumbs in a mixing bowl.

3. Rinse the halibut thoroughly. Use paper towels to dry it before baking.

4. Arrange the fish on the baking sheet. Spoon the crumbs over the fish and press it into each of the fillets.

5. Bake it until the top is browned and easily flaked or about 10 to 1minutes.

---

**Nutrition Info:**

- Calories: 273;
- Protein: 38 grams;
- Fat: 7 grams

# Syrian Spiced Lentil, Barley, And Vegetable Soup

**Servings: 5**

**Cooking Time: 40 Minutes**

**Ingredients:**

- 1 tablespoon olive oil

- 1 small onion, chopped (about 2 cups)

- 2 medium carrots, peeled and chopped (about 1 cup)

- 1 celery stalk, chopped (about ½ cup)

- 1 teaspoon chopped garlic

- 1 teaspoon ground cumin

- 1 teaspoon ground coriander

- 1 teaspoon turmeric

- ⅛ teaspoon ground cinnamon

- 2 tablespoons tomato paste

- ¾ cup green lentils

- ¾ cup pearled barley

- 8 cups water

- ¾ teaspoon kosher salt

- 1 (5-ounce) package baby spinach leaves

- 2 teaspoons red wine vinegar

**Directions:**

1. Heat the oil in a soup pot on medium-high heat. When the oil is shimmering, add the onion, carrots, celery, and garlic and sauté for 8 minutes. Add the cumin, coriander, turmeric, cinnamon, and tomato paste and cook for 2 more minutes, stirring frequently.

2. Add the lentils, barley, water, and salt to the pot and bring to a boil. Turn the heat to low and simmer for  minutes. Add the spinach and continue to simmer for 5 more minutes.

3. Add the vinegar and adjust the seasoning if needed.

4. Spoon 2 cups of soup into each of 5 containers.

5. STORAGE: Store covered containers in the refrigerator for up to days.

**Nutrition Info: Per Serving:**

- Total calories: 273;
- Total fat: 4g;
- Saturated fat: 1g;
- Sodium: 459mg;
- Carbohydrates: 50g;
- Fiber: 1;
- Protein: 12g

# Spinach Chicken

**Servings: 2**

**Cooking Time: 20 Minutes**

## Ingredients:

- 2 garlic cloves, minced

- 2 tablespoons unsalted butter, divided

- ¼ cup parmesan cheese, shredded

- ¾ pound chicken tenders

- ¼ cup heavy cream

- 10 ounce frozen spinach, chopped

- Salt and black pepper, to taste

## Directions:

1. Heat tablespoon of butter in a large skillet and add chicken, salt and black pepper.

2. Cook for about 3 minutes on both sides and remove the chicken in a bowl.

3. Melt remaining butter in the skillet and add garlic, cheese, heavy cream and spinach.

4. Cook for about 2 minutes and transfer the chicken in it.

5. Cook for about minutes on low heat and dish out to immediately serve.

6. Place chicken in a dish and set aside to cool for meal prepping. Divide it in 2 containers and cover them. Refrigerate for about 3 days and reheat in microwave before serving.

**Nutrition Info:**

- Calories: 288 ;
- Carbohydrates: 3.6g;
- Protein: 27g;

- Fat: 18.3g;
- Sugar: 0.3g;
- Sodium: 192mg

# Niçoise-style Tuna Salad With Olives & White Beans

**Servings: 4**

**Cooking Time: 20-30 Minutes**

**Ingredients:**

- Green beans (.75 lb.)

- Solid white albacore tuna (12 oz. can)

- Great Northern beans (16 oz. can)

- Sliced black olives (2.25 oz.)

- Thinly sliced medium red onion (¼ of 1)

- Hard-cooked eggs (4 large)

- Dried oregano (1 tsp.)

- Olive oil (6 tbsp.)

- Black pepper and salt (as desired)

- Finely grated lemon zest (.5 tsp.)

- Water (.33 cup)

- Lemon juice (3 tbsp.)

**Directions:**

1. Drain the can of tuna, Great Northern beans, and black olives. Trim and snap the green

beans into halves. Thinly slice the red onion. Cook and peel the eggs until hard-boiled.

2. Pour the water and salt into a skillet and add the beans. Place a top on the pot and switch the temperature setting to high. Wait for it to boil.

3. Once the beans are cooking, set a timer for five minutes. Immediately, drain and add the beans to a cookie sheet with a raised edge on paper towels to cool.

4. Combine the onion, olives, white beans, and drained tuna. Mix them with the zest, lemon juice, oil, and oregano.

5. Dump the mixture over the salad and gently toss.

6. Adjust the seasonings to your liking. Portion the tuna-bean salad with the green beans and eggs to serve.

**Nutrition Info:**

- Calories: 548;
- Protein: 36.3 grams;
- Fat: 30.3 grams

# Whole-wheat Pasta With Roasted Red Pepper Sauce And Fresh Mozzarella

---

**Servings: 4**

**Cooking Time: 40 Minutes**

---

**Ingredients:**

- 3 large red bell peppers, seeds removed and cut in half

- 1 (10-ounce) container cherry tomatoes

- 2 teaspoons olive oil, plus 2 tablespoons

- 8 ounces whole-wheat penne or rotini

- 1 tablespoon plus 1 teaspoon apple cider vinegar

- 1 teaspoon chopped garlic

- 1½ teaspoons smoked paprika

- ¼ teaspoon kosher salt

- ½ cup packed fresh basil leaves, chopped

- 1 (8-ounce) container fresh whole-milk mozzarella balls (ciliegine), quartered

**Directions:**

1. Preheat the oven to 400°F and line a sheet pan with a silicone baking mat or parchment paper.

2. Place the peppers and tomatoes on the pan and toss with teaspoons of oil. Roast for 40 minutes.

3. While the peppers and tomatoes are roasting, cook the pasta according to the instructions on the box. Drain and place the pasta in a large mixing bowl.

4. When the peppers are cool enough to handle, peel the skin and discard. It's okay if you can't remove all the skin. Place the roasted peppers,

vinegar, garlic, paprika, and salt and the remaining 2 tablespoons of oil in a blender and blend until smooth.

5. Add the pepper sauce, whole roasted tomatoes, basil, and mozzarella to the pasta and stir to combine.

6. Place a heaping 2 cups of pasta and sauce in each of 4 containers.

7. STORAGE: Store covered containers in the refrigerator for up to 5 days.

**Nutrition Info: Per Serving:**

- Total calories: 463;
- Total fat: 20g;
- Saturated fat: 7g;
- Sodium: 260mg;
- Carbohydrates: 54g;
- Fiber: 9g;
- Protein: 1

# Greek Turkey Meatball Gyro With Tzatziki

**Ingredients:**

- Turkey Meatball:

- 1 lb. ground turkey

- 1/4 cup finely diced red onion

- 2 garlic cloves, minced

- 1 tsp oregano

- 1 cup chopped fresh spinach

- Salt, to taste

- Pepper, to taste

- 2 tbsp olive oil

- Tzatziki Sauce:

- 1/2 cup plain Greek yogurt

- 1/4 cup grated cucumber

- 2 tbsp lemon juice

- 1/2 tsp dry dill

- 1/2 tsp garlic powder

- Salt, to taste

- 1/2 cup thinly sliced red onion

- 1 cup diced tomato

- 1 cup diced cucumber

- 4 whole wheat flatbreads

**Directions:**

1. In a large bowl, add in ground turkey, diced red onion, oregano, fresh spinach minced garlic, salt, and pepper

2. Using your hands mix all the ingredients together until the meat forms a ball and sticks together

3. Then using your hands, form meat mixture into 1" balls, making about 12 meatballs

4. In a large skillet over medium high heat, add the olive oil and then add the meatballs, cook each side for 3-minutes until they are browned on all sides, remove from the pan and allow it to rest

5. Allow the dish to cool completely

6. Distribute in the container, store for 2-3 days

7. To Serve: Reheat in the microwave for 1-2 minutes or until heated through. In the meantime, in a small bowl, combine the Greek yogurt, grated cucumber, lemon juice, dill,

garlic powder, and salt to taste Assemble the gyros by taking the toasted flatbread, add 3 meatballs, sliced red onion, tomato, and cucumber. Top with Tzatziki sauce and serve!

**Nutrition Info: Per Serving:**

- Calories:429;
- Carbs: 3;
- Total Fat: 19g;
- Protein: 28g

# Grilled Mediterranean Chicken Kebabs

**Servings: 10**

**Cooking Time: 10 Minutes**

**Ingredients:**

- Chicken Kebabs:

- 3 chicken fillets, cut in 1-inch cubes

- 2 red bell peppers

- 2 green bell peppers

- 1 red onion

- Chicken Kebab Marinade:

- 2/3 cup extra virgin olive oil, divided

- Juice of 1 lemon, divided

- 6 clove of garlic, chopped, divided

- 4 tsp salt, divided

- 2 tsp freshly ground black pepper, divided

- 2 tsp paprika, divided

- 2 tsp thyme, divided

- 4 tsp oregano, divided

## Directions:

1. In a bowl, mix 2 of all ingredients for the marinade- olive oils, lemon juice, garlic, salt, pepper, paprika, thyme and oregano in small bowl

2. Place the chicken in a ziplock bag and pour marinade over it, marinade in the fridge for about 30 minutes

3. In a separate ziplock bag, mix the other half of the marinade ingredients - olive oils, lemon juice, garlic, salt, pepper, paprika, thyme and oregano - add the vegetables and marinade for at least  minutes

4. If you are using wood skewers, soak the skewers in water for about 20-30 minutes

5. Once done, thread the chicken and peppers and onions on the skewers in a pattern about 6 pieces of chicken with peppers and onion in between

6. Over an outdoor grill or indoor grill pan over medium-high heat, spray the grates lightly with oil

7. Grill the chicken for about 5 minutes on each side, or until cooked through, then allow to cool completely

8. Distribute among the containers, store for 2-3 days

9. To Serve: Reheat in the microwave for 1-2 minutes or until heated through, or cover in foil and reheat in the oven at 375 degrees F for 5 minutes

10. Recipe Notes: You can also bake the Mediterranean chicken skewers in the oven. Just preheat the oven to 425 F and place the chicken skewers on roasting racks that are over two foil-lined baking sheets. Bake for 15 minutes, turn over and bake for an additional 10 - 15 minutes on the other side, or until cooked through

## Nutrition Info: Per Serving:

- Calories:228;
- Carbs: 5g;
- Total Fat: 17g;
- Protein: 14g

# Sauces and Dressings Recipes

## Antipasti Shrimp Skewers

**Servings: 4**

**Cooking Time: 10 Minutes**

**Ingredients:**

- 16 pitted kalamata or green olives

- 16 fresh mozzarella balls (ciliegine)

- 16 cherry tomatoes

- 16 medium (41 to 50 per pound) precooked peeled, deveined shrimp

- 8 (8-inch) wooden or metal skewers

## Directions:

1. Alternate 2 olives, 2 mozzarella balls, 2 cherry tomatoes, and 2 shrimp on 8 skewers.

2. Place skewers in each of 4 containers.

3. STORAGE: Store covered containers in the refrigerator for up to 4 days.

---

## Nutrition Info: Per Serving:

- Total calories: 108;
- Total fat: 6g;
- Saturated fat: 1g;
- Sodium: 328mg;

- Carbohydrates: ;
- Fiber: 1g;
- Protein: 9g

# Smoked Paprika And Olive Oil–marinated Carrots

| |
|---|
| **Servings: 4** |
| **Cooking Time: 5 Minutes** |

**Ingredients:**

- 1 (1-pound) bag baby carrots (not the petite size)

- 2 tablespoons olive oil

- 2 tablespoons red wine vinegar

- ¼ teaspoon garlic powder

- ¼ teaspoon ground cumin

- ¼ teaspoon smoked paprika

- ⅛ teaspoon red pepper flakes

- ¼ cup chopped parsley

- ¼ teaspoon kosher salt

## Directions:

1. Pour enough water into a saucepan to come ¼ inch up the sides. Turn the heat to high, bring the water to a boil, add the carrots, and cover with a lid. Steam the carrots for 5 minutes, until crisp tender.

2. After the carrots have cooled, mix with the oil, vinegar, garlic powder, cumin, paprika, red pepper, parsley, and salt.

3. Place ¾ cup of carrots in each of 4 containers.

4. STORAGE: Store covered containers in the refrigerator for up to 5 days.

---

**Nutrition Info: Per Serving:**

- Total calories: 109;
- Total fat: 7g;
- Saturated fat: 1g;
- Sodium: 234mg;
- Carbohydrates: 11g;
- Fiber: 3g;
- Protein: 2g

# Tzatziki Sauce

**Ingredients:**

- 1 English cucumber

- 2 cups low-fat (2%) plain Greek yogurt

- 1 tablespoon olive oil

- 2 teaspoons freshly squeezed lemon juice

- ½ teaspoon chopped garlic

- ½ teaspoon kosher salt

- ⅛ teaspoon freshly ground black pepper

- 2 tablespoons chopped fresh dill

- 2 tablespoons chopped fresh mint

**Directions:**

1. Place a sieve over a medium bowl. Grate the cucumber, with the skin, over the sieve. Press the grated cucumber into the sieve with the flat surface of a spatula to press as much liquid out as possible.

2. In a separate medium bowl, place the yogurt, oil, lemon juice, garlic, salt, pepper, dill, and mint and stir to combine.

3. Press on the cucumber one last time, then add it to the yogurt mixture. Stir to combine. Taste and add more salt and lemon juice if necessary.

4. Scoop the sauce into a container and refrigerate.

5. STORAGE: Store the covered container in the refrigerator for up to days.

---

**Nutrition Info:Per Serving (¼ cup):**

- Total calories: 51;

- Total fat: 2g;
- Saturated fat: 1g;
- Sodium: 137mg;
- Carbohydrates: 3g;
- Fiber: <1g;
- Protein: 5g

# Fruit Salad With Mint And Orange Blossom Water

**Ingredients:**

- 3 cups cantaloupe, cut into 1-inch cubes

- 2 cups hulled and halved strawberries

- ½ teaspoon orange blossom water

- 2 tablespoons chopped fresh mint

**Directions:**

1. In a large bowl, toss all the ingredients together.

2. Place 1 cup of fruit salad in each of 5 containers.

3. STORAGE: Store covered containers in the refrigerator for up to 5 days.

---

## Nutrition Info: Per Serving:

- Total calories: 52;
- Total fat: 1g;
- Saturated fat: <1g;
- Sodium: 10mg;
- Carbohydrates: 12g;
- Fiber: 2g;
- Protein: 1g

# Soups and Salads Recipes

## Minestrone Soup

Servings: 6

Cooking Time: 25 Minutes

## Ingredients:

- 2 tablespoons olive oil

- 3 cloves garlic, minced

- 1 onion, diced

- 2 carrots, peeled and diced

- 2 stalks celery, diced

- 1 1/2 teaspoons dried basil

- 1 teaspoon dried oregano

- 1/2 teaspoon fennel seed

- 6 cups low sodium chicken broth

- 1 (28-ounce can diced tomatoes

- 1 (16-ounce can kidney beans, drained and rinsed

- 1 zucchini, chopped

- 1 (3-inch Parmesan rind

- 1 bay leaf

- 1 bunch kale leaves, chopped

- 2 teaspoons red wine vinegar

- Kosher salt and black pepper, to taste

- 1/3 cup freshly grated Parmesan

- 2 tablespoons chopped fresh parsley leaves

**Directions:**

1. Preheat olive oil in the insert of the Instant Pot on Sauté mode.

2. Add carrots, celery, and onion, sauté for 3 minutes.

3. Stir in fennel seeds, oregano, and basil. Stir cook for 1 minute.

4. Add stock, beans, tomatoes, parmesan, bay leaf, and zucchini.

5. Secure and seal the Instant Pot lid then select Manual mode to cook for minutes at high pressure.

6. Once done, release the pressure completely then remove the lid.

7. Add kale and let it sit for 2 minutes in the hot soup.

8. Stir in red wine, vinegar, pepper, and salt.

9. Garnish with parsley and parmesan.

10.  Enjoy.

---

**Nutrition Info:**

- Calories: 805;
- Carbohydrate: 2.5g;
- Protein: 124.1g;
- Fat: 34g;

- Sugar: 1.4g;
- Sodium: 634mg

# Kombu Seaweed Salad

| |
|---|
| **Servings: 6** |
| **Cooking Time: 40 Minutes** |

**Ingredients:**

- 4 garlic cloves, crushed

- 1 pound fresh kombu seaweed, boiled and cut into strips

- 2 tablespoons apple cider vinegar

- Salt, to taste

- 2 tablespoons coconut aminos

**Directions:**

1. Mix together the kombu, garlic, apple cider vinegar, and coconut aminos in a large bowl.

2. Season with salt and combine well.

3. Dish out in a glass bowl and serve immediately.

## Nutrition Info:

- Calories: 257;
- Carbs: 16.9g;
- Fats: 19.;
- Proteins: 6.5g;
- Sodium: 294mg;
- Sugar: 2.7g

# Desserts Recipes

## Almond Shortbread Cookies

| Servings: 16 |
| :---: |
| Cooking Time: 25 Minutes |

**Ingredients:**

- ½ cup coconut oil

- 1 teaspoon vanilla extract

- 2 egg yolks

- 1 tablespoon brandy

- 1 cup powdered sugar

- 1 cup finely ground almonds

- 3 ½ cups cake flour

- ½ cup almond butter

- 1 tablespoon water or rose flower water

**Directions:**

1. In a large bowl, combine the coconut oil, powdered sugar, and butter. If the butter is not soft, you want to wait until it softens up. Use an electric mixer to beat the ingredients together at high speed.

2. In a small bowl, add the egg yolks, brandy, water, and vanilla extract. Whisk well.

3. Fold the egg yolk mixture into the large bowl.

4. Add the flour and almonds. Fold and mix with a wooden spoon.

5. Place the mixture into the fridge for at least 1 hour and 30 minutes.

6. Preheat your oven to 325 degrees Fahrenheit.

7. Take the mixture, which now looks like dough, and divide it into 1-inch balls.

8. With a piece of parchment paper on a baking sheet, arrange the cookies and flatten them with a fork or your fingers.

9. Place the cookies in the oven for 13 minutes, but watch them so they don't burn.

10.  Transfer the cookies onto a rack to cool for a couple of minutes before enjoying!

---

**Nutrition Info:**

- calories: 250,
- fats: 14 grams,

- carbohydrates: 30 grams,
- protein: 3 grams.

# Chocolate Fruit Kebabs

**Servings: 6**

**Cooking Time: 30 Minutes**

**Ingredients:**

- 24 blueberries

- 12 strawberries with the green leafy top part removed

- 12 green or red grapes, seedless

- 12 pitted cherries

- 8 ounces chocolate

**Directions:**

1. Line a baking sheet with a piece of parchment paper and place 6, -inch long wooden skewers on top of the paper.

2. Start by threading a piece of fruit onto the skewers. You can create and follow any pattern that you like with the ingredients. An example pattern is 1 strawberry, 1 cherry, blueberries, 2 grapes. Repeat the pattern until all of the fruit is on the skewers.

3. In a saucepan on medium heat, melt the chocolate. Stir continuously until the chocolate has melted completely.

4. Carefully scoop the chocolate into a plastic sandwich bag and twist the bag closed starting right above the chocolate.

5. Snip the corner of the bag with scissors.

6. Drizzle the chocolate onto the kebabs by squeezing it out of the bag.

7. Put the baking pan into the freezer for 20 minutes.

8. Serve and enjoy!

## Nutrition Info:

- calories: 254,
- fats: 15 grams,
- carbohydrates: 28 grams,
- protein: 4 grams.

# Meat Recipes

## Spicy Chicken Breasts

**Servings: 6**

**Cooking Time: 30 Minutes**

**Ingredients:**

- 1 ½ pounds chicken breasts

- 1 bell pepper, deveined and chopped

- 1 leek, chopped

- 1 tomato, pureed

- 2 tablespoons coriander

- 2 garlic cloves, minced

- 1 teaspoon cayenne pepper

- 1 teaspoon dry thyme

- 1/4 cup coconut aminos

- Sea salt and ground black pepper, to taste

**Directions:**

1. Rub each chicken breasts with the garlic, cayenne pepper, thyme, salt and black pepper.

Cook the chicken in a saucepan over medium-high heat.

2. Sear for about 5 minutes until golden brown on all sides.

3. Fold in the tomato puree and coconut aminos and bring it to a boil. Add in the pepper, leek, and coriander.

4. Reduce the heat to simmer. Continue to cook, partially covered, for about 20 minutes.

5. Storing

6. Place the chicken breasts in airtight containers or Ziploc bags; keep in your refrigerator for 3 to 4 days.

7. For freezing, place the chicken breasts in airtight containers or heavy-duty freezer bags. It will maintain the best quality for about 4 months. Defrost in the refrigerator. Bon appétit!

## Nutrition Info:

- 239 Calories;
- 6g Fat;
- 5.5g Carbs;
- 34.3g Protein;
- 1g Fiber

# Saucy Boston Butt

**Servings: 8**

**Cooking Time: 1 Hour 20 Minutes**

## Ingredients:

- 1 tablespoon lard, room temperature

- 2 pounds Boston butt, cubed

- Salt and freshly ground pepper

- 1/2 teaspoon mustard powder

- A bunch of spring onions, chopped

- 2 garlic cloves, minced

- 1/2 tablespoon ground cardamom

- 2 tomatoes, pureed

- 1 bell pepper, deveined and chopped

- 1 jalapeno pepper, deveined and finely chopped

- 1/2 cup unsweetened coconut milk

- 2 cups chicken bone broth

## Directions:

1. In a wok, melt the lard over moderate heat. Season the pork belly with salt, pepper and mustard powder.

2. Sear the pork for 8 to 10 minutes, stirring periodically to ensure even cooking; set aside, keeping it warm.

3. In the same wok, sauté the spring onions, garlic, and cardamom. Spoon the sautéed vegetables along with the reserved pork into the slow cooker.

4. Add in the remaining ingredients, cover with the lid and cook for 1 hour 10 minutes over low heat.

5. Storing

6. Divide the pork and vegetables between airtight containers or Ziploc bags; keep in your refrigerator for up to 3 to 5 days.

7. For freezing, place the pork and vegetables in airtight containers or heavy-duty freezer bags. Freeze up to 4 months. Defrost in the refrigerator. Bon appétit!

---

**Nutrition Info:**

- 369 Calories;
- 20.2g Fat;
- 2.9g Carbs;
- 41.3g Protein;
- 0.7g Fiber

# Old-fashioned Goulash

**Servings: 4**

**Cooking Time: 9 Hours 10 Minutes**

**Ingredients:**

- 1 ½ pounds pork butt, chopped

- 1 teaspoon sweet Hungarian paprika

- 2 Hungarian hot peppers, deveined and minced

- 1 cup leeks, chopped

- 1 ½ tablespoons lard

- 1 teaspoon caraway seeds, ground

- 4 cups vegetable broth

- 2 garlic cloves, crushed

- 1 teaspoons cayenne pepper

- 2 cups tomato sauce with herbs

- 1 ½ pounds pork butt, chopped

- 1 teaspoon sweet Hungarian paprika

- 2 Hungarian hot peppers, deveined and minced

- 1 cup leeks, chopped

- 1 ½ tablespoons lard

- 1 teaspoon caraway seeds, ground

- 4 cups vegetable broth

- 2 garlic cloves, crushed

- 1 teaspoons cayenne pepper

- 2 cups tomato sauce with herbs

**Directions:**

1. Melt the lard in a heavy-bottomed pot over medium-high heat. Sear the pork for 5 to 6

minutes until just browned on all sides; set aside.

2. Add in the leeks and garlic; continue to cook until they have softened.

3. Place the reserved pork along with the sautéed mixture in your crock pot. Add in the other ingredients and stir to combine.

4. Cover with the lid and slow cook for 9 hours on the lowest setting.

5. Storing

6. Spoon your goulash into four airtight containers or Ziploc bags; keep in your refrigerator for up to 3 to 4 days.

7. For freezing, place the goulash in airtight containers. Freeze up to 4 to 6 months. Defrost in the refrigerator. Enjoy!

**Nutrition Info:**

- 456 Calories;
- 27g Fat;
- 6.7g Carbs;
- 32g Protein;
- 3.4g Fiber

# Flatbread With Chicken Liver Pâté

| |
|---|
| **Servings: 4** |
| **Cooking Time: 2 Hours 15 Minutes** |

## Ingredients:

- 1 yellow onion, finely chopped

- 10 ounces chicken livers

- 1/2 teaspoon Mediterranean seasoning blend

- 4 tablespoons olive oil

- 1 garlic clove, minced

- For Flatbread:

- 1 cup lukewarm water

- 1/2 stick butter

- 1/2 cup flax meal

- 1 ½ tablespoons psyllium husks

- 1 ¼ cups almond flour

## Directions:

1. Pulse the chicken livers along with the seasoning blend, olive oil, onion and garlic in your food processor; reserve.

2. Mix the dry ingredients for the flatbread. Mix in all the wet ingredients. Whisk to combine well.

3. Let it stand at room temperature for 2 hours. Divide the dough into 8 balls and roll them out on a flat surface.

4. In a lightly greased pan, cook your flatbread for 1 minute on each side or until golden.

5. Storing

6. Wrap the chicken liver pate in foil before packing it into airtight containers; keep in your refrigerator for up to 7 days.

7. For freezing, place the chicken liver pate in airtight containers or heavy-duty freezer bags. Freeze up to 2 months. Defrost overnight in the refrigerator.

8. As for the keto flatbread, wrap them in foil before packing them into airtight containers; keep in your refrigerator for up to 4 days.

9. Bon appétit!

**Nutrition Info:**

- 395 Calories;
- 30.2g Fat;
- 3.6g Carbs;
- 17.9g Protein;
- 0.5g Fiber

# Sunday Chicken With Cauliflower Salad

| Servings: 2 |
| --- |
| Cooking Time: 20 Minutes |

**Ingredients:**

- 1 teaspoon hot paprika

- 2 tablespoons fresh basil, snipped

- 1/2 cup mayonnaise

- 1 teaspoon mustard

- 2 teaspoons butter

- 2 chicken wings

- 1/2 cup cheddar cheese, shredded

- Sea salt and ground black pepper, to taste

- 2 tablespoons dry sherry

- 1 shallot, finely minced

- 1/2 head of cauliflower

**Directions:**

1. Boil the cauliflower in a pot of salted water until it has softened; cut into small florets and place in a salad bowl.

2. Melt the butter in a saucepan over medium-high heat. Cook the chicken for about 8 minutes or until the skin is crisp and browned. Season with hot paprika salt, and black pepper.

3. Whisk the mayonnaise, mustard, dry sherry, and shallot and dress your salad. Top with cheddar cheese and fresh basil.

4. Storing

5. Place the chicken wings in airtight containers or Ziploc bags; keep in your refrigerator for up 3 to 4 days.

6. Keep the cauliflower salad in your refrigerator for up 3 days.

7. For freezing, place the chicken wings in airtight containers or heavy-duty freezer bags. Freeze up to 3 months. Once thawed in the refrigerator, reheat in a saucepan until thoroughly warmed.

---

**Nutrition Info:**

- 444 Calories;
- 36g Fat;
- 5.7g Carbs;
- 20.6g Protein;
- 4.3g Fiber

# Sides & Appetizers Recipes

## Olive Tuna Pasta

**Servings: 4**

**Cooking Time: 20 Minutes**

## Ingredients:

- 8 ounces of tuna steak, cut into 3 pieces

- ¼ cup green olives, chopped

- 3 cloves garlic, minced

- 2 cups grape tomatoes, halved

- ½ cup white wine

- 2 tablespoons lemon juice

- 6 ounces pasta - whole wheat gobetti, rotini, or penne

- 1 10-ounce package frozen artichoke hearts, thawed and squeezed dry

- 4 tablespoons extra-virgin olive oil, divided

- 2 teaspoons fresh grated lemon zest

- 2 teaspoons fresh rosemary, chopped, divided

- ½ teaspoon salt, divided

- ¼ teaspoon fresh ground pepper

- ¼ cup fresh basil, chopped

**Directions:**

1. Preheat grill to medium-high heat.

2. Take a large pot of water and put it on to boil.

3. Place the tuna pieces in a bowl and add 1 tablespoon of oil, 1 teaspoon of rosemary, lemon zest, a ¼ teaspoon of salt, and pepper.

4. Grill the tuna for about 3 minutes per side.

5. Transfer tuna to a plate and allow it to cool.

6. Place the pasta in boiling water and cook according to package instructions.

7. Drain the pasta.

8. Flake the tuna into bite-sized pieces.

9. In a large skillet, heat remaining oil over medium heat.

10. Add artichoke hearts, garlic, olives, and remaining rosemary.

11. Cook for about 3-4 minutes until slightly browned.

12. Add tomatoes, wine, and bring the mixture to a boil.

13. Cook for about 3 minutes until the tomatoes are broken down.

14. Stir in pasta, lemon juice, tuna, and remaining salt.

15. Cook for 1-2 minutes until nicely heated.

16. Spread over the containers.

17. Before eating, garnish with some basil and enjoy!

## Nutrition Info: Per Serving:

- Calories: 455,
- Total Fat: 21.2 g,
- Saturated Fat: 3.5 g,
- Cholesterol: 59 mg,
- Sodium: 685 mg,
- Total Carbohydrate: 38.4 g,
- Dietary Fiber: 6.1 g,
- Total Sugars: 3.5 g,
- Protein: 25.5 g,
- Vitamin D: 0 mcg,
- Calcium: 100 mg,
- Iron: 5 mg,
- Potassium: 800 mg

# Braised Artichokes

**Servings: 6**

**Cooking Time: 30 Minutes**

## Ingredients:

- 6 tablespoons olive oil

- 2 pounds baby artichokes, trimmed

- ½ cup lemon juice

- 4 garlic cloves, thinly sliced

- ½ teaspoon salt

- 1½ pounds tomatoes, seeded and diced

- ½ cup almonds, toasted and sliced

## Directions:

1. Heat oil in a skillet over medium heat.

2. Add artichokes, garlic, and lemon juice, and allow the garlic to sizzle.

3. Season with salt.

4. Reduce heat to medium-low, cover, and simmer for about 15 minutes.

5. Uncover, add tomatoes, and simmer for another 10 minutes until the tomato liquid has mostly evaporated.

6. Season with more salt and pepper.

7. Sprinkle with toasted almonds.

8. Enjoy!

---

## Nutrition Info: Per Serving:

- Calories: 265,
- Total Fat: 1g,
- Saturated Fat: 2.6 g,
- Cholesterol: 0 mg,
- Sodium: 265 mg,

- Total Carbohydrate: 23 g,
- Dietary Fiber: 8.1 g,
- Total Sugars: 12.4 g,
- Protein: 7 g,
- Vitamin D: 0 mcg,
- Calcium: 81 mg,
- Iron: 2 mg,
- Potassium: 1077 mg

# Great Mediterranean Diet Recipes

## Tofu And Vegetable Provençal

| Servings: 4 |
| --- |
| Cooking Time: 30 Minutes |

**Ingredients:**

- 1 pound super-firm tofu, cut into ¾-inch cubes

- 2 tablespoons freshly squeezed lemon juice

- 2 tablespoons olive oil

- 1 teaspoon garlic powder

- 1 teaspoon herbes de Provence

- ¼ teaspoon kosher salt

- 4 teaspoons olive oil, divided

- 1 (14-ounce) eggplant, cubed into 1-inch pieces (5 to 6 cups)

- 1 small yellow onion, chopped (about 2 cups)

- 2 teaspoons chopped garlic

- 10 ounces cherry tomatoes, halved if tomatoes are fairly large

- 1 (14-ounce) can artichoke hearts, drained

- 1 teaspoon herbes de Provence

- ¼ teaspoon kosher salt

- ½ cup dry white wine, such as sauvignon blanc

- ⅓ cup pitted kalamata olives, roughly chopped

- 1 (½-ounce) package fresh basil, chopped

**Directions:**

1. TO MAKE THE TOFU

2. Place the tofu in a container with the lemon juice, oil, garlic powder, herbes de Provence, and salt. Allow to marinate for 1 hour.

3. When you're ready to cook the tofu, preheat the oven to 400°F and line a sheet pan with a silicone baking mat or parchment paper. Lift the tofu out of the marinade and place it on the sheet pan. Bake for  minutes, flipping the tofu

over after 15 minutes. Cool, then place about ½ cup of tofu cubes in each of 4 containers.

4. TO MAKE THE VEGETABLE RAGOUT

5. While the tofu is marinating, heat 2 teaspoons of oil in a 12-inch skillet over medium-high heat. When the oil is shimmering, add the eggplant and cook for 4 minutes, stirring occasionally. Remove the eggplant and place on a plate.

6. Add the remaining 2 teaspoons of oil to the pan, and add the onion and garlic. Cook for 2 minutes. Add the tomatoes and cook for 5 more minutes. Add the eggplant, artichokes, herbes de Provence, salt, and wine. Cover the pan, lower the heat, and simmer for 20 minutes.

7. Turn the heat off and stir in the olives and basil.

8. Spoon about 1½ cups of vegetables into each of the 4 tofu containers.

9. STORAGE: Store covered containers in the refrigerator for up to 5 days.

---

**Nutrition Info: Per Serving:**

- Total calories: 362;
- Total fat: 17g;
- Saturated fat: 3g;
- Sodium: 728mg;
- Carbohydrates: 32g;
- Fiber: 9g;
- Protein: 23g

# Banana, Orange, And Pistachio Smoothie

## Ingredients:

- 1 (17.6-ounce) container plain low-fat (2%) Greek yogurt

- 3 very ripe medium bananas

- 1½ cups orange juice

- ¾ cup unsalted shelled pistachios

## Directions:

1. Place all the ingredients in a blender and blend until smooth.

2. Pour 1¾ cups of the smoothie into each of 3 smoothie containers.

3. STORAGE: Store covered containers in the refrigerator for up to 4 days.

**Nutrition Info: Per Serving:**

- Total calories: 9;
- Total fat: 19g;
- Saturated fat: 4g;
- Sodium: 71mg;
- Carbohydrates: 55g;
- Fiber: 3g;
- Protein: 26g

# Breakfast Bento Box

**Servings: 2**

**Cooking Time: 12 Minutes**

**Ingredients:**

- 2 eggs

- 2 ounces sliced prosciutto

- 20 small whole-grain crackers

- 20 whole, unsalted almonds (about ¼ cup)

- 2 (6-inch) Persian cucumbers, sliced

- 1 large pear, sliced

**Directions:**

1. Place the eggs in a saucepan and cover with water. Bring the water to a boil. As soon as the

water starts to boil, place a lid on the pan and turn the heat off. Set a timer for  minutes.

2. When the timer goes off, drain the hot water and run cold water over the eggs to cool. Peel the eggs when cool and cut in half.

3. Place 2 egg halves and half of the prosciutto, crackers, almonds, cucumber slices, and pear slices in each of 2 containers.

4. STORAGE: Store covered containers in the refrigerator for up to 5 days.

**Nutrition Info: Per Serving:**

- Total calories: 370;
- Total fat: 20g;
- Saturated fat: ;
- Sodium: 941mg;
- Carbohydrates: 35g;
- Fiber: 7g;
- Protein: 16g

# Maple-cardamom Chia Pudding With Blueberries

Servings: 5

Cooking Time: 5 Minutes

## Ingredients:

- 2½ cups low-fat (2%) milk

- ½ cup chia seeds

- 1 tablespoon plus 1 teaspoon pure maple syrup

- ¼ teaspoon ground cardamom

- 2½ cups frozen blueberries

## Directions:

1. Place the milk, chia seeds, maple syrup, and cardamom in a large bowl and stir to combine.

2. Spoon ½ cup of the mixture into each of 5 containers.

3. Place ½ cup of frozen blueberries in each container and stir to combine. Let the pudding sit for at least an hour in the refrigerator before eating.

4. STORAGE: Store covered containers in the refrigerator for up to 5 days.

---

**Nutrition Info: Per Serving:**

- Total calories: 218;
- Total fat: 8g;
- Saturated fat: 2g;
- Sodium: 74mg;
- Carbohydrates: 28g;
- Fiber: 10g;
- Protein: 10g

# Cheesy Bread

**Ingredients:**

- 3 cups shredded cheddar cheese

- 1 cup mayonnaise

- 1 1-ounce pack dry ranch dressing mix

- 1 2-ounce can chopped black olives, drained

- 4 green onions, sliced

- 2 French baguettes, cut into ½ inch slices

**Directions:**

1. Preheat oven to 350 degrees Fahrenheit.

2. In a medium-sized bowl, combine cheese, ranch dressing mix, mayonnaise, onions, and olives.

3. Increase mayo if you want a juicier mixture.

4. Spread cheese mixture on top of your French baguette slices.

5. Arrange the slices in a single layer on a large baking sheet.

6. Bake for about 15 minutes until the cheese is bubbly and browning.

7. Cool and chill.

8. Serve warm!

**Nutrition Info: Per Serving:**

- Calories: 2,
- Total Fat: 17 g,
- Saturated Fat: 7.2 g,
- Cholesterol: 35 mg,

- Sodium: 578 mg,
- Total Carbohydrate: 23.9 g,
- Dietary Fiber: 1.1 g,
- Total Sugars: 2.4 g,
- Protein: 11.1 g,
- Vitamin D: 3 mcg,
- Calcium: 229 mg,
- Iron: 2 mg,
- Potassium: 85 mg

# Conclusion

This is the best way to lose weight and stay fit. Tastefully eat healthy and natural products, mixed in fantastic recipes.

Talk to a certified nutritionist before starting any diet or nutritional plan and have them follow you through this fantastic Mediterranean adventure.

While you continue to eat these delicious meals get some physical activity too.

Thank you so much for reading my book I look forward to future recipes.

CPSIA information can be obtained
at www.ICGtesting.com
Printed in the USA
BVHW061034220321
603178BV00004B/298